Words

A simple reflection

Amy Churchouse

**First published in 2020 by
Doing Things Differently**

The words in this book will take you off an adventure. An adventure which may take you in many different directions, all of which you are encouraged to explore, if you so wish. It may bring realisations and new perspectives. Some of the questions may have answers for you that are interesting and others that are challenging.

This journey is yours and will deliver what you allow it to. Please take your time and proceed with curiosity. Reflect and explore with compassion and without judgment. Discover what might be possible with new awareness and a deeper understanding. These words have been written to create opportunities. Where they take you will depend on how you engage with them.

And they all start with a simple reflection...

Words.

What do they do for us?
What do they do to us?

Where do they take us and
what do they bring us?

What would we have
and what would we do,
if they were taken away?

So many words.

What do they mean?
And to who and why?

Where did we pick them up, learn about what they mean and how
does that change the way we feel about them?

Or the people they are attached to.

What do they tell people about us?
And are they right?

So simple, a combination of letters.
Yet they carry so much expectation, power and responsibility.
So much potential for understanding.

And for misunderstanding...

Do they speak the truth?
Or do they only describe someone's perspective?

Do we believe them? And why is that?

Because we trust them?
Or because we trust who said them?

Because we understand?
And how do we know we understand...?

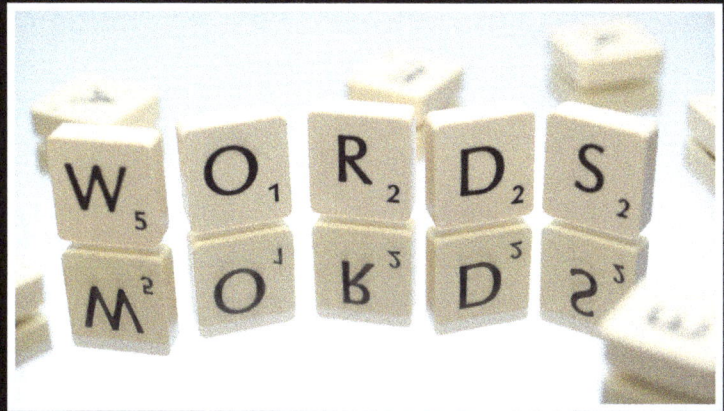

Before there were words
there were humans.

What would happen if we
took the words away?

What does that say about you?

What can I know about you when you introduce yourself?

Mr, Mrs or Ms?

How would you describe yourself?

To yourself?

And to others?

What words would you use?
What do they mean to you?
And what do they mean to me?

Why did you choose those words?

Did someone tell you you were strong, weak, smart or a geek?
Did that become a part of the description?

Or a part of your human?

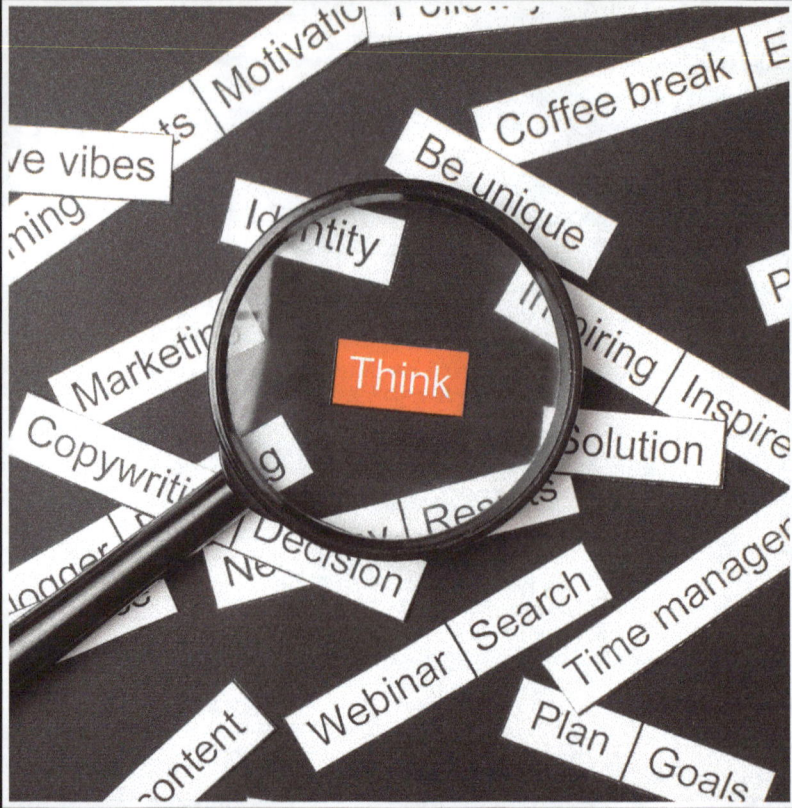

Before there were words
there were humans.

What would happen if we
took the words away?

What are the labels you wear?

Were they given to you, attached by you,
or assumed by others based on how you are?
Or how you appear?

Do they do a good job telling everyone about you?

Or do they unintentionally package you with other things?
With other people?

And are those other people really like you?

Are these labels words you use because then other people know?
Will they know you?

Or are these labels you choose because it helps them to
understand?

Because you are proud?

Because these words make you feel strong?
Because they protect you?
Because it makes things easier?

Easier for you or only for them?

Feminist, activist, anarchist?
Unionist, patriot...?

Do these words mean they're angry?
Up for a fight?

Or passionate? Or stubborn? Or staunch? Committed?
Or maybe they got hurt?

Do these words help us to connect with them?
To learn? To understand?

Or does that depend on how these words are worn?
Or who is wearing them?

dis·ci·pline[1] /'dɪs
, does not o
mind and charact
of obedience

Professional, corporate, tradie?
Unemployed, volunteer...?

Description? Label? Vocation?
Or just words?

Which one are you and what does that say about you?

What opportunities does it offer you?
Or maybe take away from you?

Does it say that you're smart? Or skilled?
Or stupid? Or lazy?
That you like working hard?

Or does it depend on who you are talking to?
And who they know?

And what they know?
About you...

Or what they know about being professional, corporate,
a tradie, unemployed or a volunteer.

Before there were words
there were humans.

What would happen if we
took the words away?

evil
justice
trust
life
decision
concern
code
ETHICS
philosophy
morals
wrong
right
choices
question
?
dilemma
good
bad

Feelings are words.

What is that you are feeling?

Do you describe it as anxiety?
Or excitement? Or energy?
Or is it adrenalin?

Angry. Sad. Happy. Scared?

How do you feel when you say that is how you are feeling?

Does using that word make you feel good or bad?
Better or worse?

What do you decide to do with that?
And how do you know what to do?

Did someone's words help you know?

"How are you?"

FINE

confused betrayed useless
broken
never good enough
fragile anxious i'm falling apart and
you don't notice it
pathetic annoying rejected
lonely
defeated

How do you feel when someone uses these words?

Anxiety, depression, trauma, survivor...

Maybe a doctor?
Or a friend?
Or your mother?

Do you believe them?
Do you believe what you feel? Or what you see?

How do you know what to believe?

Gay, straight, bi, queer, asexual, lesbian?

Do they tell your story? Or state your position?

Or is it just a description?
Does it matter?

Why is that?

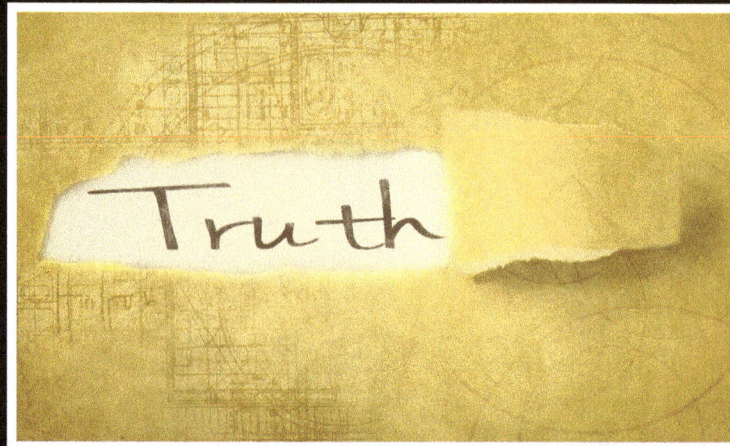

How much of your story do these words share?

Did they get you kicked out of home?
Married three times?
Pregnant too young?

Did they make you like sport? Trucks or dolls?
Or want to have kids?

Do they describe how you like to connect?
To touch or to hold?

Or who you want to connect with?
Someone, everyone, anyone?
Or no one?

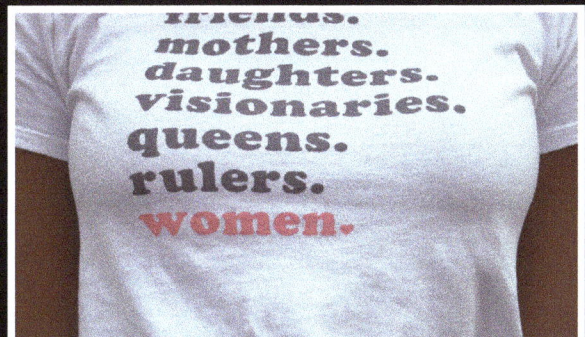

friends.
mothers.
daughters.
visionaries.
queens.
rulers.
women.

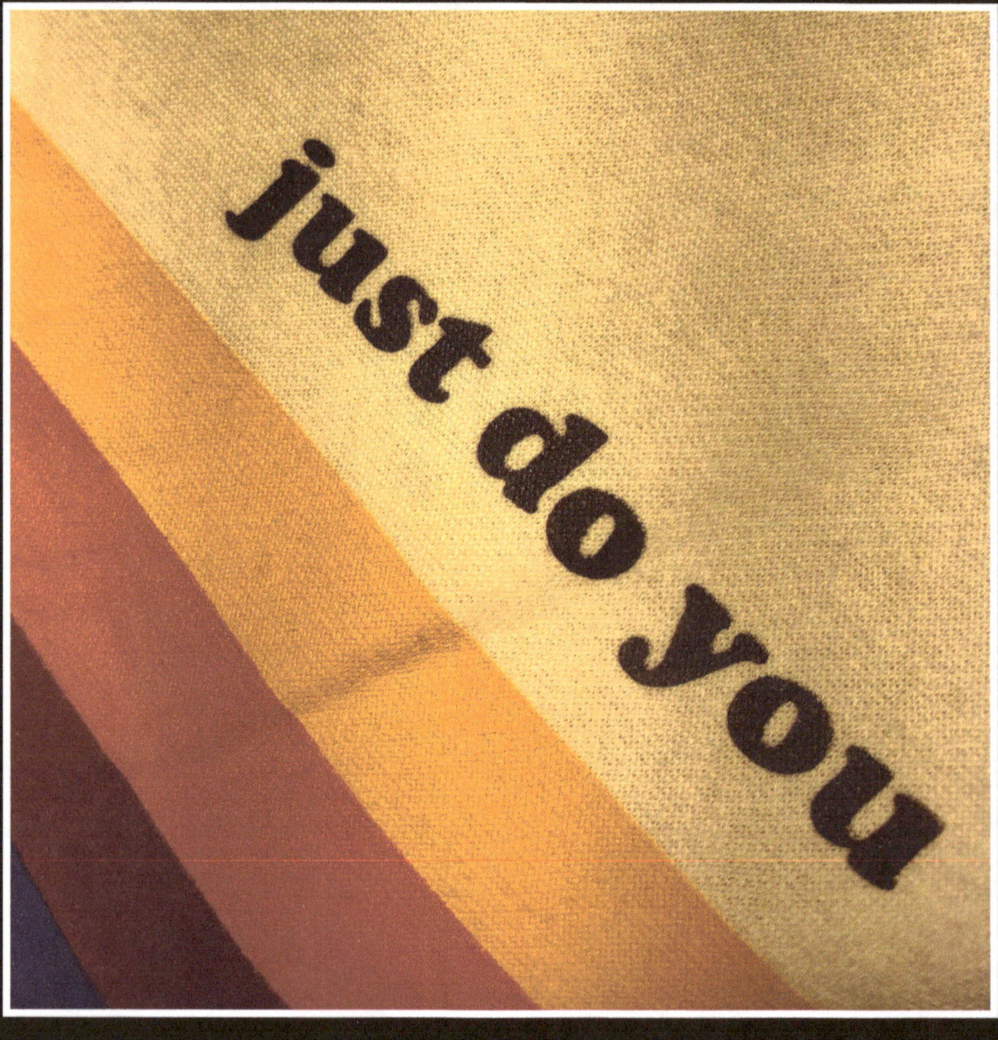
just do you

Monogamous.

Polyamorous.

How many and why?
Now or back then or forever?

How do you know and why is that so?

Do these words create boundaries for you?
Or barriers for others? Or both?
How does that work for you?

Have you thought about how it might be to wear the other word?
To explore the other word?

If you did, would you use the word?
And what new words would you need to know to do so?

Before there were words
there were humans.

What would happen if we
took the words away?

I
COULD KILL YOU RIGHT
THROUGH YOUR PIERCING
HEART BITING STABING
SWALLOW THEM WHOLE TAKE YOUR POISON
SPITFUL CLAWING GROWLING CUTTING
HIT YOU IN THE CHEST LEAD IN
YOUR
GUT WICKED VILE HATEFUL
EVIL MURDER TEAR BETTER
BABY RUN
I'LL
YOU TO PIECES
WATCH ME
BRING YOU DOWN
YOUR LIFE IS IN MY HANDS
YOU'RE DEAD
SCREAM DEATH
ALL YOU WANT IN YOUR
BONES
TEARING I'LL BE
THE END
BYE SAY OF YOU
BABY
RIPPING YOU YOUR
APART
PRAYERS

Safe.

What does that mean?
And who to?

Will you be safe?
Is that place safe?
And what makes it so?
According to who?

Perhaps you mean what are the risks?

And then don't the risks depend on the person?

How much they know?
And how big they are?
Who they are connected with and what skills they have?

If we are 'safe', or they are 'safe' or somewhere is 'safe', what does that mean we can do?

How do we engage?

With confidence?

With no fear?

Do we question?

Are we open?

Curious?

Paying attention?

Staying aware?

Are we really safe?

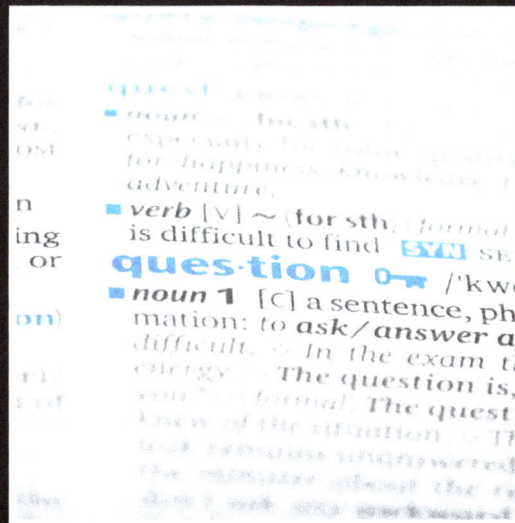

Tolerate it? Or resent it?

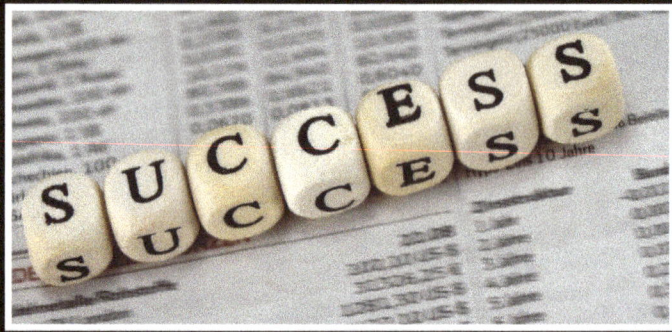

Is it learning?

Growing? Creating? Exploring? Questioning?
Progress? Contribution? Determination? Pain? Improvement?
Connection? Belonging?

Security?

Are you sure?

Do you work for the pay?
The puzzle?
The power?
Or the prestige?

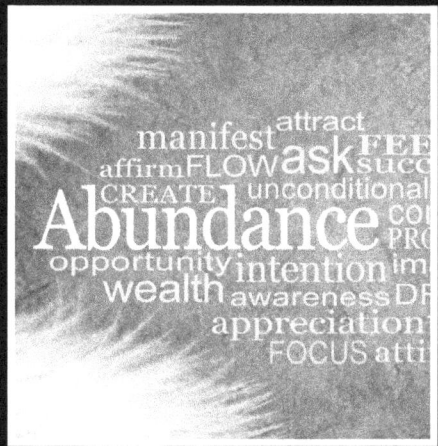

DO IT
Live LOVE Laugh
Freshly Brewed
Classic Italian Coffee
How Great would life be if we lived a little of it Everyday
ENJOY THIS DAY
Be present
BREATHE DEEPLY
Show gratitude
BE FEARLESS
TRY NEW THINGS
MY KIDS HAVE PAWS
LOVE
friends are the stars that light up your life
COUNT YOUR BLESSINGS
when nothing goes right... Go Left
WAKE UP SAY A PRAYER AND HUSTLE
LIFE BEGINS AFTER COFFEE
EVERYDAY is a fresh start
GOOD MOMS HAVE STICKY FLOORS, DIRTY OVENS, AND HAPPY KIDS.
HAPPY WIFE HAPPY LIFE
DREAMS DON'T WORK UNLESS YOU DO
Family is all the love you need
IF YOUR DREAMS DON'T SCARE YOU THEY'RE NOT BIG ENOUGH
Live them
All our dreams can come true

Before there were words
there were humans.

What would happen if we
took the words away?

UNDENIABLE
sweetheart lips
craving NEVERENDING relationship
extravagant WEDDING &
RAPTURE lust seek TRUST new ENJOY SPARK
enchant
emotion CARE fond feeling red
devote & affection PURE hot
ETERNAL CRUSH magic moments
AMOUR LOST SUGAR passion commitment GOOD
SADNESS FOREVER
longing purple ONE kiss favour playful
fond unrestrained infatuation
intense strong ave
care Your big ROMANCE
LOVE
ecstatic TRUST PROPOSE promise sensual TOUCH
POTENTIAL MARRY I'm sorry RENDEZVOUS GESTURE hold
gain BABY FANTASY vulnerable mate
fire caress spouse ALLWAYS goodbye
beau NEVER MEMORY
BOY honey kid COUPLE CHERISH
favoured warm hands soulmate
perfect gift EMOTIONS MOTIVES SAFETY
life receive divine inclination
HEARTBEAT
you
SUNSHINE first
groom
JOY DATING AFFAIR
provacative involvement
NOW FUTURE
FOREVER! PURPOSE
bride CONNECTION
beauty exotic FOND
OPEN SEX SUGAR GRACE
TRUST DENIAL BLISS
arousing attachment loveable
REVEALING TRUTH
HONEYMOON PAIN TOUCH
FEEL seductive
SOFT teardrop
EMBER delicate
companion FLAME
DARLING SOFT
girlfriend

Love.

Can you see it when you look at them?
When they do what they do?

Do you feel it?
When you do what you do?

Or is it just a word that you use?

I love you.

What does that mean?
When you say it?
When you hear it?

Or are they just some words that we say...?

Before there were words
there were humans.

What would happen if we
took the words away?

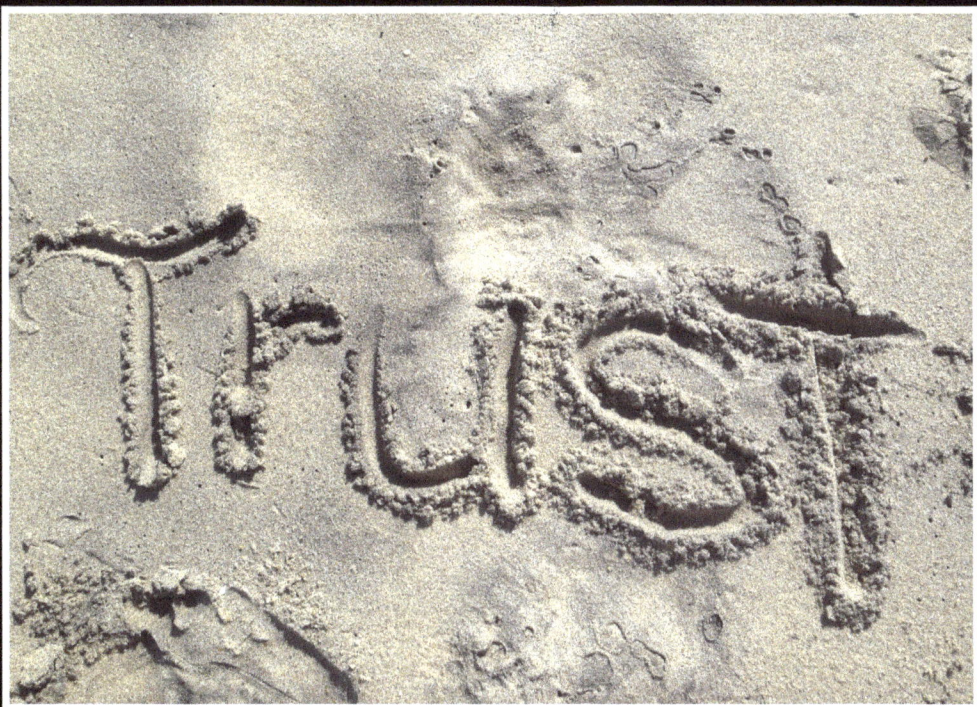

Or alienate us.

Will they soothe or scar?
And how long for?

Words.

They are all just words.

Words I understand, and you understand.

Sometimes.

But often we don't, and then we don't know.
And then we don't know what to do.
Don't know how to feel, how to be...

Or what to say.

Before there were words
there were humans.

What would happen if we
took the words away?

Words Have Power

Epilogue

Where did these words take you?

Did they make you think about the words you use?
Or those that others choose?
About their depth and diversity of meaning?

About how they make you feel?
About how yours might be heard by other people?

About how damaging a misunderstanding can be?
And how unnecessary these are when they begin at the words?

About what words can achieve? Or destroy?

Did it make you want to learn more words?
Or to know what is behind the words?
Will you now explore further, listen closer or look deeper...?

What would you do if there were no words?
How would you connect?
How would you share?
How would you learn and how would you know?

www.ingramcontent.com/pod-product-compliance
Lightning Source LLC
Chambersburg PA
CBHW061243030426
42338CB00011B/1325